# MiSS MARY

# MiSS MARY

## THE IRISH WOMAN WHO SAVED THE LIVES OF HUNDREDS OF CHILDREN DURING WORLD WAR II

### Bernard S. Wilson
### Illustrated by Julia Castaño

*Gill Books*

Gill Books
Hume Avenue
Park West
Dublin 12
www.gillbooks.ie

Gill Books is an imprint of M.H. Gill and Co.

Text © Bernard S. Wilson 2020
Illustrations © Julia Castaño 2020
978 0 7171 8655 6

Designed by iota (www.iota-books.ie)
Proofread by Djinn von Noorden

Printed and bound in Great Britain
by Clays Ltd, Elcograf S.p.A.
This book is typeset in Poynter

The paper used in this book comes from
the wood pulp of managed forests. For
every tree felled, at least one tree is planted,
thereby renewing natural resources.

A CIP catalogue record for this book is
available from the British Library.

5 4 3 2 1

*Dedicated to Rosemary Bailey (1953–2019). Rosemary was a dear friend, and the first person to write about Mary Elmes.*

# CONTENTS

IRELAND

•Dublin

•Cork

GREAT
BRITAIN

•London

FRANCE

•Paris

Toulouse

Rivesaltes•

•Marseille

Argelès-sur-Mer• •Perpignan
and Canet Plage

SPAIN

•Madrid

•Polop

Alicante•

•Torremolinos

•Gibraltar

N

# CHAPTER ONE

# FRANCINE'S LETTER

FRANCINE WAS HUNGRY. VERY HUNGRY. **And** she wasn't the only one. All the children – and the grown-ups too – in the French village where she lived were hungry and they were starting to get sick. But why was this? What had happened to Francine and all the other hungry people?

There was a war going on – the Second World War. It began in September 1939, when Great Britain and France declared war on Germany because Germany, led by an evil man named Hitler, had invaded Poland. At first, the war seemed far away to Francine, but in May 1940, things got really bad. Hitler's armies invaded France and, in 39 days, Francine's country had lost. The people of France were now suffering as a result. Most of the men were prisoners of war. This meant that they were not allowed to return to their homes, so there was no one to work in the fields. Even if there had been, only grapes, tomatoes and other fruits were grown in Francine's village, and you can't live on fruit alone. The people needed bread and milk and vegetables to stay strong and healthy, and these things were not available.

There was nothing for breakfast in Francine's home except coffee. Now, French people don't usually eat large breakfasts.

They would usually have delicious croissants, which they would dip into big bowls of coffee. They might have some fruit and cheese as well. Even children drink coffee in France. Francine could remember those mouth-watering pastries and warm drinks, but these days the coffee didn't taste like it used to. People were making it from acorns, and there were certainly no croissants now. So that's all that Francine could have for breakfast that morning, before she went to school. It was hard to drag herself along the lane every day when she was so hungry, and even harder to concentrate on doing sums. But soon it would be midday, and Francine knew that midday meant food.

Yes, there was going to be a school dinner that day, and probably the next day too. And hopefully every day for the rest of that week.

This was because Miss Mary had been with her sacks of chickpeas, lentils and rice, and her barrel of oil. The school cook would be able to make a lovely soup with these things. Francine could almost smell it already. And maybe, just maybe, Miss Mary would have brought some of her treats, too, like chocolate, or even a spoonful of jam! Francine's mouth watered at the thought of it.

A few days earlier, Francine and the other children in her class had written letters to Miss Mary, to thank her for what she did for them. Francine had started her letter, 'Dear Miss Mary', but her teacher said that she must not call her that – not in a letter, anyway. Instead, she must call her 'Mademoiselle', the French word for 'Miss'. This is what Francine wrote:

· ● ·

Dear Mademoiselle,

All of the pupils in my school, even the littlest ones, know your name – Miss Elmes. Those words will always remind us of snacks that we have been without for so long: chocolate and jam. Thank you so much for all that we owe you.

Francine Delmas, aged 9

· ● ·

Francine's teacher had said that she should really have thanked Miss Mary for the soup, as that was what was going to give her the strength she needed. And the crispy bread roll that each child had been given too. But she had allowed Francine to keep the letter as it was. Francine's teacher knew that the treats were important as well, and it was so kind of Miss Mary to bring those little gifts that brought them such happiness in these dreadful times.

# CHAPTER TWO

# THE ADVENTURE BEGINS

SO WHO WAS MISS MARY? How was she able to feed these children? What was her story?

Mary was Irish. She was born in 1908 in a lovely home in Ballintemple, Cork. Her father, Edward Elmes, was a pharmacist in the family business, J. Waters & Sons, and he owned a shop in the centre of Cork city. Her mother, Elizabeth Elmes, was a remarkable woman. She worked hard to get equal rights for women at the time. Mary had a wonderful childhood. She had a younger brother, John, who kept her company. Their parents always encouraged them to ask questions and explore the world around them.

When Mary was eight years old, she went to one of the best schools in Cork, Rochelle School, just down the road from where she lived. Mary loved school, and for the next 20 years, Mary's life was one of study. First at school in Cork, then at Trinity College, Dublin, and then at the London School of Economics. She spent a year in France, near Paris, visiting all the sights and writing about what she saw in her diary – all in perfect French. She also spent some time in Madrid, where she came to love Spain and the Spanish people. She did brilliantly at school, and by 1937, when she was nearly 30, everyone thought she was ready for a big career in business, or even the Irish civil service.

When Mary was studying in London, she had met a rich Englishman named Sir George Young. He had worked for many years in Spain and had written several books about the country. Like Mary, he loved the Spanish people and everything that made Spain so different and special – the amazing buildings, the wonderful countryside, the warm weather, the music and dancing. Now there was a war happening in Spain, and Sir George was worried about the children there.

All across Spain, towns and villages were being attacked and people were getting injured. Sometimes even the children were getting hurt. Even though Sir George was paying for ambulances to be sent to Spain, some of the injuries were so bad that not everyone survived. Sir George's wife, Lady Young, was looking for nurses and doctors to leave their work in England and go to Spain to help her husband.

Mary wanted to help. But she wasn't a doctor or a nurse, so it didn't seem possible for her to do anything useful. But Sir George did have a job for her. At the time, two young Spanish girls were living and working in his home in England. They were worried about what was happening in Spain and wanted to go home. Lady Young was going to Spain soon, so it was decided that the girls would go with her on a ship to Gibraltar. But Sir George needed someone who could take them from Gibraltar into Spain and on to their home in Torremolinos. He asked Mary if she would do this and she agreed. This would be her opportunity to get into Spain and help the children who were being hurt by this terrible war.

On 13 February 1937, Mary, Lady Young and the two Spanish girls sailed from London on the SS *Otranto* and arrived in Gibraltar two days later. After Mary brought the two girls safely to their home, she wondered how she could help next. Her travel papers only allowed her to stay in Spain for five days, and two of those had passed already. She knew about a group of trained nurses that had come out to Gibraltar to help Sir George. Would they let her join them to do what she could? She decided to try.

Back in Gibraltar, Mary met the nurses and offered to help them.

'What can you do?' they asked her. 'Are you a trained nurse? Are you a doctor?'

'No,' said Mary.

'Well, would you be able to drive an ambulance?'

Mary had to admit that she wasn't able to do any of these things. 'But I can speak Spanish and French very well,' she said. 'Wouldn't that be a help?'

•  ●  •

The nurses looked at each other. What could they say? What could they do? They had a lot of organising to do. Perhaps she could be useful in some way.

Finally, they agreed: 'Yes, we'll find something for you to do.'

•  ●  •

Mary was so pleased. She was sure that she could make herself useful and she was glad that she was going to stay on longer than she expected. But Mary had no idea of the adventures she was about to have or the dangers she would have to face. She didn't know that it would be over two years, not five days, before she went back to Ireland.

# CHAPTER THREE

# THE CHILDREN OF SPAIN

PALMIRA'S MOTHER WAS STANDING in the town square in Alicante. The square was packed with people going about their business. The men were hurrying to their offices to work and the women, like Palmira's mother, were shopping for the day's meals. Children were running around everywhere, playing and laughing with each other. They all knew there was the danger of an explosion at any moment, because they were in the middle of a war. But life had to go on, money had to be earned and food had to be bought.

At that moment it happened! A shell from a ship out in the bay landed right in the square and exploded. Palmira, who was not yet two years old, was blown out of her mother's arms and landed on the ground. She got some terrible injuries. Her left leg and foot were badly hurt. When the doctors examined her, they thought that she might never be able to walk. But another doctor, called Doctor Blanc, believed that with careful nursing Palmira's foot might be saved. He knew about a hospital up in the mountains, near a town called Polop, where there were nurses who took in children like Palmira.

●  ●  ●

He knew that if anyone could provide the care and love that Palmira needed, the lady in charge of the hospital would do it. That lady was Mary – our Miss Mary – although she wasn't called that yet.

●  ●  ●

Mary had been a great success since she came to Spain. Her knowledge of the Spanish people and her ability to speak Spanish had been such a help to Sir George's nurses and doctors that she was now in charge of the hospital in the mountains. It was just a big empty house when Mary got there, and she had turned it into a wonderful place for wounded children like Palmira to come and find love and care. After a few months of careful treatment, Palmira was able to stand, then take a few steps, and finally she was able to walk again. Doctor Blanc had been right to bring the little girl to Mary's hospital, and thanks to Mary and her nurses, Palmira's foot was saved. Everyone was so happy about Palmira's recovery, especially when her father arrived. He had been searching for her for months. At last he found her alive and well, and he was able to take her home.

Not every story had a happy ending. Mary's nurses worked so hard, but some of the children brought to Mary's hospital were so badly injured, or so sick and hungry, that they could not be saved. One little boy was found wandering on a battlefield by himself.

He was too young to know his name or where his parents were. He didn't know where his home was, either. He was brought to Polop, where he was loved and cared for by all the staff. He kept saying the word 'Tato', so that is what they decided to call him. He grew to love Mary deeply, and she thought about adopting him. But it was difficult to get permission from the Spanish authorities when nobody knew who he was, and Mary was unable to go ahead with her wishes. Another boy, Pepe, made Mary a lovely card for New Year's Day, 1938. It meant so much to her that she kept it for the rest of her life.

Around this time, Mary got some sad news from home. Her father had died suddenly and her mother wanted her to come home for the funeral. Mary started to make plans to return to Ireland, but she had to find someone to take her place. Her nurses were very good at their jobs, but they couldn't speak Spanish like Mary. She knew she couldn't leave them to run the entire hospital alone, so Mary wrote to her mother to say she couldn't come home. As much as Mary loved her parents, she couldn't leave the children in the hospital, where no one spoke Spanish well enough to care for them properly.

CHAPTER FOUR

# ON THE
# BEACH

MARY DID EVENTUALLY COME HOME. **The fighting in Spain had ended, Mary's hospital had been closed and it was time for Mary and all the nurses to leave.**

Of course, Mary was glad to be back in Cork with her mother. Together they went to visit her father's grave. Mary was sad that she hadn't been able to say goodbye to him. But Mary's thoughts were still with her Spanish friends. What had happened to them? She was soon to find out.

The stories were in all of the newspapers. A terrible man named General Franco had taken control of the country and, rather than stay in Spain, many people chose to escape to France. There were photos of families struggling to pass through the mountains that divided Spain from France. It was the middle of winter and there was snow and ice everywhere. It was said that half a million people had made this terrible journey on foot, and now many of them were huddled together on the beaches with nowhere for shelter and nothing to eat. What was to become of them?

Mary knew that something had to be done, and she knew that she had to help.

One day, she told her mother:

*   ●   *

'I have to go to France to help these people!'

'But Mary,' her mother replied, 'you've only just got home. You said you'd only be gone about five days the last time and you were gone two years! How long is it going to be this time?'

*   ●   *

'I don't know,' said Mary. 'As long as it takes, I suppose. Someone has to organise things on those beaches. I'm going to offer to do just that. They may not want me, but I must offer.'

In fact, Mary was badly needed. Because of all the wonderful work she had done in organising things in the hospitals in Spain, Mary was the perfect person to help take charge of the situation. Mary's job was to bring joy to these poor people. Others could organise shelters and food supplies, but Mary was to provide the things that make life fun.

Things like footballs, skipping ropes and toys for the children. Pencils and paper, crayons, blackboards and easels, too, so that some kind of school could be set up. And for the grown-ups, musical instruments, paints and paintbrushes, tools and even a small library.

Mary spent some time in Paris ordering all the things she needed. They would be sent on later, but she hurried down to the beaches in the south of France as quickly as she could, where all these people were.

She was shocked by what she saw. Some rough shelters had been built from driftwood brought up by the sea, but many, even mothers and children, had no shelter at all. Mary had to find somewhere for herself to live and she had to gather a team to help her, but her main task, every day, was to visit these poor people on the beach. She talked to them and listened to their needs, and she tried to bring them something to give them courage and hope. This is when people first started to call her 'Miss Mary'.

Soon everyone, not only on the beach where she worked but all along the coast, knew of Miss Mary, her kindness and her love. They made her little gifts, beautiful figures made out of wood or bone and carved with some of the tools she had provided. The children made her lovely paintings, many of which she kept and treasured.

One man named Agusti Bartra was on another beach, farther down the coast. He hoped to get on a boat and go to Mexico, but he knew he would have to wait a while before that could happen. Agusti was a writer and a poet, and he thought it would be useful if he used his time on the beach to learn English. But he needed a Spanish–English dictionary. How could he find one when he wasn't allowed to leave the beach? Someone told Agusti about Miss Mary, so he wrote to her. A few days later a parcel arrived for him. It was a Spanish–English dictionary, but it wasn't a new one. Mary hadn't been able find one anywhere. This was France and all the dictionaries she could find were in French. She had sent him her own dictionary!

It was the only one she had, the one she had used when she was a student in Dublin and in London. It even had her name in it.

Agusti talked about it years later, when he was safely in Mexico. He said that he took it with him wherever he went. He thought it was a sign of real love and he would never forget Miss Mary, even though he had never met her.

Mary settled down in a house in Perpignan, a city in the south of France, near the Spanish border. She set up her office there too. She didn't know it at the time, but it would be six years before she saw Ireland or her mother again.

# CHAPTER FIVE

# FEEDING THE CHILDREN

—◄•●•►—

DO YOU REMEMBER FRANCINE? The little girl who wrote to Mary, telling her that everyone in her school knew her name? Well, now you know a lot more about Mary – Miss Mary, as the children called her. But how did Mary manage to find the food that Francine and her friends so badly needed?

Mary was now working for the American Quakers. Quakers are a religious group who believe in caring for people in trouble.

Whenever there is a war, a lot of people suffer. A lot of ordinary people get hurt. Ordinary men, women and children are sometimes made homeless, hungry and ill, and people like the Quakers are there to help. Mary was not a Quaker herself, but she was happy to work for them because she also cared about people in trouble, especially children.

Mary received money and food from America and it was her job to see that it was put to good use. She organised food supplies to be sent throughout the south of France. Sadly, there wasn't enough for everybody, so she had to make sure the youngest children were fed first. The easiest way to do this was to send the food to the schools. The teachers could supervise the feeding. Mary also asked them to weigh the children every week, to make sure they were getting enough.

* ● *

Mary visited the schools as often as she could to check that everything was being done properly. Of course, there were babies to think of too, and the babies were too young to go to school. So Mary organised places in towns and villages where milk and baby food could be handed out.

In this way, Mary saved the lives of thousands of babies and children.

* ● *

As if this wasn't difficult enough, Mary had another problem to solve. Do you remember all the people from Spain who had left their homes and travelled across the mountains to France? People like this are called refugees. At first, these poor people had been left all alone on the beaches to get by as best they could, but by now they were being settled into camps. They had buildings to live and sleep in, but they weren't very comfortable. They had to go outside to use the toilet and the camps weren't very clean. There was some food provided, but not enough for everyone and people were often hungry. Mary visited these camps as often as she could. She realised that she had to find a way to feed the children in these camps, as well as the French children in their homes and schools.

## FEEDING THE CHILDREN

Mary knew that she had to get these children out of the camps. There was very little for them to do all day, nowhere to wash properly and so little to eat. She had to find places up in the mountains or down by the sea where the children could relax and enjoy life again. Where they could be washed and given new clean clothes. Where they could sleep in proper beds and eat proper meals, just as they had done before the war came and upset their lives. Because of the war, there were lots of big houses lying empty, and Mary thought they would make wonderful holiday homes for these children.

Mary got permission from the authorities to take some of them out of the camp, as long as she promised to bring them back shortly. This meant she had to ask for the parents' permission to take their children away from the camp. It was not an easy decision for them to make. But hundreds of children got to enjoy a month or two away from the camps. Then they would go back to their parents to make room for another group of children.

# CHAPTER SIX

# A BIG DECISION

MARY LOOKED AT THE ENVELOPE that had arrived on her desk. She knew she had to make up her mind quickly, because time was running out. Really, her mind was made up already. She knew what she wanted to say. But was she sure that this was the right thing to do?

Inside the envelope was a letter from her boss, Howard Kershner. He was the person in charge of the AFSC in France. AFSC stands for 'American Friends' Service Committee'. This was the organisation that was sending the money, food and equipment that Mary and her team were using to help the victims of the war in her area.

As we have seen, Mary was very busy and had a lot to do. She had to see that the French children in her area were getting enough food. She also had to worry about the children and their parents in all the camps that had sprung up along the coast. We know from the letters she wrote that she was finding all this work very difficult to manage. It was a full-time job, and there was no time for holidays because the problems never went away.

The biggest problem for Mary was the camps. It was December and it was bitterly cold. The wind, which was called the Tramontane, blew over the camps day after day from the icy mountains. It was freezing. Most people only had the clothes they arrived with. There was no heating in the buildings where they lived and slept. The water supply was also dirty and this meant a terrible disease called typhus was spreading through some of the camps. It made people very sick, and old people and babies were in danger of dying. When Mary returned to her comfortable home after a day visiting the camps, she felt bad for leaving all these people there. She felt guilty that she had a warm bed and a healthy meal waiting for her at home. These people had done nothing wrong. They should be back in their own homes. Mary wanted to do more for these people.

Mary sighed and picked up the letter on her desk. She read it again. Her boss was telling her that he and his wife were going back to America soon. Someone else would have to take over his work, but he needed someone to do his wife's work too. She was responsible for organising the children's 'colonies'. These were the homes that had been opened in the mountains or by the sea, where children could take a break from the awful camps for a couple of months. Howard was asking Mary if she would leave the many things she was working on and concentrate on running these colonies. Mary would be based in Marseille, a big city in the south of France. She would have to travel to each colony to make sure everything was being done properly, that the children were comfortable, clean and well fed. It was a nice, safe job. There was no risk of her becoming ill, and no need to spend hours in the dirty camps. She started to write her reply:

'I feel greatly honoured that you should feel that I am qualified to carry on the work of the Colony Department for Mrs Kershner.'

But Mary went on to explain that she felt her duty was to remain in the job she had, looking after all the refugees in the camps. She said that she was known by all the people in the camps, and that even when they were suddenly moved from one camp to another, they knew that she would still be there to visit them in their new surroundings and would help them settle in as best they could. She said:

* ● *

I think that it is a little encouragement to some of them to know that I continue to be interested in them after two and a half years. I hope that you will understand the point of view that I have tried to show above, and that you will forgive me for not falling in with your very kind suggestion.

* ● *

Did she make the right decision? Let's find out.

# CHAPTER SEVEN

# THE TRAINS KEEP COMING

—◂•●•▸—

HANS FREUND AND HIS FAMILY had been in a camp called Rivesaltes for about two weeks. They had tried to leave France by crossing into Switzerland but they had been arrested and sent to this camp. There were four of them in the family: Hans, his wife, Eva, and their two little boys, Michael, who was six, and Ronald, who was two. Hans was an engineer. He designed motorcars. He and his family were from Germany and he had taught engineering in a university there. His wife was a doctor. The family had moved to Italy, where Michael was born, and then to France, where Ronald was born. They had to keep moving because they were Jewish and, sadly, Jewish people were being treated terribly in many countries across Europe.

France was known for being a friendly country, where everyone was welcome. There had even been a law that made it illegal to print unkind things in books and newspapers about people with different religions and beliefs. But when France was defeated in the war, all this changed. People who had been made welcome when fleeing their own country were now being forced into these terrible camps. Rivesaltes was one of the worst camps. The laws were changed so that not only could people say unkind things about Jewish people, they were encouraged to do so! Rivesaltes was full of people who had done nothing wrong. They had committed no crime. They were simply among the people that the new government hated. There were also Spanish refugees, Jehovah's Witnesses, Gypsies and people of different races and religions, that the government treated badly, in these camps. The government called them 'undesirables'.

Rivesaltes was not just one big camp. It was made up of a lot of smaller camps. Each camp was surrounded by barbed wire. Families were divided between these camps. Women and children were kept together in some parts, and men and boys over the age of 14 were kept in other parts. But things had started to change recently. All the Jewish men, women and children were brought together in one part of the camp. They were told that this was because it would be easier for them to celebrate the season of Passover together.

•  ●  •

But trains had started to come to the camps, and people noticed that it was just the Jewish people, Gypsies and the Jehovah's Witnesses who were being loaded onto them and sent away to unknown places.

•  ●  •

Mary, and other workers in the different organisations, had a plan. They were already taking children out of the camps so they could have a break from the terrible conditions there. But, of course, the children had to be brought back.

Mary's plan worked like this. Mary wanted to ask mothers to sign a form that allowed her and workers like her to take the children out of the camps and keep them until things returned to normal. When the camps were closed and people were allowed to return to their own countries and their own homes, then the children would be reunited with their parents. Mary had a horrible feeling that some of the mothers and fathers being sent away on the trains would never be coming back. So Mary was really asking these mothers to say goodbye to their children forever. But could she tell them that? Of course not!

It was a terrible task for Mary. Mary loved the children so much. She knew how much danger the children were in and she had to save them. She had to take these little boys and girls away from their mothers, knowing that they might never see each other again, yet she couldn't tell them.

Hans Freund had the same thought as Mary. He was worried that he and his family would be put on the next train, and he felt that it would be bad news if they were. The trains had been coming and going for several months now. The people who went on these trains simply disappeared. They were never heard from again. Hans wrote to his friends in America and England and asked them to do what they could to help. If they couldn't help him and his wife, could they help to save his sons, Michael and Ronald?

Mary Elmes knew about Hans and his family. She had visited them in the camp a few times and she already had plans to take the children away to safety. So when she received a telegram from her boss's office in Marseille asking if she could do something to help the family get out of Rivesaltes, she wasted no time.

That same evening, on 26 September 1942, Mary drove to the camp and took Michael and Ronald in her car to a beautiful home in the mountains for children like them. Records show that, when they got there, they were quickly sent to a hospital in Perpignan because they were very sick from the poor conditions in the camp. But then the records tell no more. The boys simply vanished.

This sounds like bad news, but it wasn't. It was actually good news – very good news. It meant that Michael and Ronald had been taken into hiding. They were safe at last. Miss Mary had saved them just in time!

But what happened to Michael and Ronald's parents, Hans and Eva Freund? Sadly, Hans Freund was put on one of the trains. The train took him to Poland, where he was one of the six million people murdered simply because they were Jewish.

* ● *

But Eva, the boys' mother, was spared, perhaps because she was a doctor and useful in the camps. In time, Eva was able to join the boys in a small French village and when the war eventually ended, they all made their way to England, and then on to Canada and America.

* ● *

We now know that 2,251 Jewish people were sent from Rivesaltes on the trains, first to Paris, and then on to Poland, where almost all of them were killed. Among these were 110 children, but without the help of Mary Elmes – Miss Mary – and the kind people she worked with in other organisations, there would have been many more children on those trains. We don't know how many children people like Mary saved, but it must have been hundreds.

# CHAPTER EIGHT

# CHARLOTTE'S STORY

ONE OF THE CHILDREN MARY SAVED was a girl called Charlotte. Charlotte Berger was just five years old when a terrible thing happened. Charlotte was separated from her mother, and her mother was taken away. Charlotte would never forget it.

Charlotte had been with her mother in Rivesaltes, the same camp that Hans Freund and his family would arrive in a few days later. It was a day when one of the trains left the camp, full of people who had done nothing wrong except that they happened to be Jewish. That meant that they had to go, and Charlotte's mother was one of them. We don't know why Charlotte didn't have to go as well, but we do know that the very next day, Miss Mary came to find her. With two other little girls, Mary took Charlotte to a lovely house right by the sea, only a few miles away. There Charlotte met many other children who, just like her, had been separated from their parents. This house was called the Villa Saint Christophe, and it had been chosen by Mary as a very nice place to take children from the camp at Rivesaltes. There were two American ladies in charge of the Villa. They belonged to a religious group called the Mennonites and they worked together with Mary to save many Jewish children.

When the train carrying Charlotte's mother reached a station called Montauban, there were several people waiting for it on the platform. They had been told that the train was coming and that the poor people on it would need food and water. These people at the station were, like Mary, working with the Quakers, and they came with water and rice to feed the hungry and thirsty people on the train. It was a very hot day and these people needed water badly.

Many of the people on the train had written messages on scraps of paper, which they passed out to the Quaker workers. These pieces of paper contained messages to friends and relations, and were probably the last messages that these people would ever receive from their loved ones. Charlotte's mother was one of those who managed to send a message in this way. It was addressed to Charlotte and it said:

* ● *

Tell Charlotte that I send her my most affectionate thoughts and a thousand kisses!

* ● *

The Quaker workers in Montauban had been told that Charlotte would be taken to a big house many miles away in the middle of France. This is where the message was sent. But Mary had actually taken Charlotte to the Villa by the sea, so she never got the message. Some years later, Charlotte was sent to that big house in the middle of France, but it was too late. The message had been lost and Charlotte never knew about it.

Seventy-five years later, when she was living in Paris and now quite an elderly woman, Charlotte had a visitor. It was a lady from Ireland named Clodagh Finn. Clodagh was writing a book about Mary. She had found Charlotte's name in the archives she was studying and wanted to interview Charlotte about her time in the camp, and to ask her what she remembered about Mary. It was only after Clodagh got back to Ireland that she discovered the message from Charlotte's mother in the same archives.

        ●     ●     ●

'I must show this to Charlotte as soon as possible!' Clodagh thought.

        ●     ●     ●

So Clodagh flew back to Paris the very next day and showed Charlotte the message from her mother that she had never got to read. Can you imagine what that must have felt like for Charlotte? To read that her mother had sent her kisses all those years ago and she had never known?

That's not the end of the story. There is a building in Paris called the Holocaust

Museum. It had been set up to remember the terrible things that had been done during the war, and Charlotte had been there many times. She knew that the Holocaust Museum would be interested in all of this. She went to the museum and told her story to the people who worked there. They were very interested, and they told her that they would add it to their files of facts and stories about those who had been rescued all those years before.

Just as Charlotte was about to leave the museum, one of the ladies there said:

*   *   *

'Wait a minute! I think we have something else that will interest you.'

*   *   *

She went away and, a few minutes later, returned with something in her hand, which she passed to Charlotte. 'Look what we have found in our records,' she said.

It was a photograph of Charlotte's mother. Charlotte had never seen a photo of her mother and could barely remember what she had looked like. Now she knew. What a wonderful day! Charlotte had just received a thousand kisses from the mother she hardly remembered, and now she had her photograph, too.

# CHAPTER NINE

# WHERE HAVE THEY TAKEN MARY?

IT WAS A COLD WINTER'S DAY and **Mary** was working in her office in her home in Perpignan. There was a knock on the front door. It was more than a knock. It was somebody banging really hard. Mary looked up from her work. Her secretary was downstairs, and she would go to open the door to see who was making all this fuss. There was shouting too. Something was surely wrong. Mary got up and moved to the window, which looked down on the street below. There was a black car parked outside. That explained everything: the German police were here.

For some time now, things had been different in Perpignan. Even though most of France was still under the control of Germany, the southern area of France, where Mary worked, had not yet been occupied by German soldiers. But that had all changed recently. Now there were German soldiers and tanks everywhere and Mary had to be very careful about what she did. The big camp of Rivesaltes was closed now. There were no more Jewish families there that needed her help. But there were many Jewish children hidden in the homes she was responsible for, like the one in the mountains where she had taken Michael and Ronald. These children needed to be protected. To save them from being put on the trains that had been coming every week to take the Jewish people away, Mary and her friends had been busy changing the children's names on their identity cards and moving them to other places where they wouldn't be found. This was dangerous work. It was against the law to help anybody escape from France, and that's exactly what they were trying to do.

Mary watched as the policemen searched her office and the rooms where she lived. She knew that there were papers that would get her into serious trouble if they were found. But Mary had hidden them very carefully, and she was sure they wouldn't find them. Eventually the men gave up their search. They hadn't found anything, but they arrested Mary and took her away all the same. Her secretary knew what to do. They had made plans for an emergency like this. They hoped it would never happen, but it had and now they had to act. The American Quakers had offices in other big towns in the south of France, including their headquarters in Marseille. They must all be warned. They couldn't just ring up their colleagues and tell them what had happened. The plan was to send a message in code. We don't know what it was, but it might have been something like 'Happy birthday!' or 'Many happy returns of the day!' So this is what they did, and soon everyone knew that the worst had happened – that Mary had been taken prisoner.

A few days later, Mary's secretary was told that Mary had been taken to the prison in Toulouse. This was another big town about 200 kilometres from Perpignan. There was a

Quaker office in Toulouse, too, and Mary had good friends there: Helga Holbek, who came from Denmark, and Alice Resch, a young Norwegian nurse. They were told the news about Mary, and Helga and another friend lost no time in going to the prison to ask if they could see her. Eventually they were allowed to bring Mary things that she would need if she was going to be held in prison, and every few days they brought her parcels of food and other things that she asked for.

Mary's friends and colleagues did everything they could to get her released. They wrote to the government officials, pointing out that Mary was from Ireland, that she had an Irish passport, and that Ireland was not involved in this war between Germany and Great Britain. But then they received more bad news. Mary had suddenly vanished. She was no longer in the prison in Toulouse. The officials there said that she had been transferred to a big prison just outside Paris, hundreds of kilometres away. But the officials at this prison, called Fresnes, said that they had no record of her being there. She certainly hadn't escaped. If she had, somebody would have been around to her office to look for her and ask questions. So, where was she?

Back in Cork, Mary's mother was becoming very worried indeed. Nobody had told her that her daughter was in prison because the family doctor had said that she was too old and too ill to be told such a thing. He was afraid that the shock would kill her. But Mary's mother had heard nothing from her daughter for well over a year, and she couldn't understand why nobody seemed to be doing anything about it. Finally, the news somehow reached her. It didn't kill her. Instead, it made her very angry. She found out that her son John had known for some time that Mary was in prison, but he hadn't told her. Mary's mother had some important friends in Ireland and America, and she started to write at once to these people who she thought might be able to help.

* ● *

She had fought all her life for equal rights, and she wasn't going to keep quiet now just because she was old and ill. If it was possible to get news of her daughter, she was determined she would get it.

* ● *

Then the news came from Paris that Mary had been found. Well, really, she had never been lost. It was just her name that had gone missing! It was all a mistake about the spelling of her name. In French, a 'H' at the beginning of a word is not pronounced, just like 'hour' in English, which is pronounced like 'our'. Because Mary's name was pronounced 'Elmes', the prison authorities thought that her name was spelled like 'Helmes'. They had been looking for someone whose name began with a 'H' and not with an 'E'. What a mess! But Mary was found, arrangements were made for someone to visit her and permission was given for food parcels to be sent to her.

• ● •

We don't know what happened to Mary when she was in prison. She never spoke about it. Even years later, she never mentioned that time when she was locked up. When asked about her time there, she once replied:

'Well, we all suffered some incon- venience in those days, didn't we!'

• ● •

But after Mary had been in prison for six months, she was suddenly released. Her friends wanted her to take a rest and go to Switzerland or Portugal, countries that were neutral like Ireland, and countries where she could not get into any more trouble. But Mary insisted on returning to her office in Perpignan and carrying on with her work in feeding and caring for all the children who needed her help, who loved her and called her 'Miss Mary'.

# CHAPTER TEN

# A HAPPY ENDING

AT LAST THE WAR IN EUROPE WAS OVER! **The** prisoners of war were coming home, and France – the whole of the country – was free again. There was great celebration everywhere, but there was one place in the south of France where the joyful celebrations were also a little bit sad. Mary Elmes was leaving. Miss Mary, loved by children and grown-ups alike, was finishing her work with the American Quakers in Perpignan. She was going to get married.

It was Friday, 7 June 1946. All of Mary's friends, all the people she had worked with through those dangerous times during the war, from her deputy to the ladies who did the cleaning, were there to say goodbye. Although the war was over, food was still rationed, and it was very difficult to obtain many things. But, somehow, they had managed to put together a real feast of goodies, including a banquet of pastries made from flour, which they had been storing up for weeks for this special occasion.

Señor Rafel, who had looked after the management of Mary's office, made a lovely speech in Spanish saying how much all the Spanish workers had enjoyed working for Mary and how grateful the Spanish refugees were for her sympathy, as well as how understanding she was of their problems.

These were people who had been driven out of Spain nearly ten years previously, who Mary had rescued from the beaches and to whom she had given jobs.

Mary thanked Señor Rafel for his kind words, but she also asked if she could correct him.

*　●　*

The Spanish workers had not worked *for* her, she said. They had worked *together*, as friends.

*　●　*

She really hoped that they would be able to go back to their own homes in Spain soon, and that she was looking forward to visiting them there. Afterwards, one of the secretaries there said that she had never seen so many eyes filled with tears and that Mary was greatly loved and admired by all who knew her. She added that the memory of Miss Mary would always be in their thoughts and minds.

A few days later, on 12 June 1946, Mary Elmes and Roger Danjou were married in the town hall of Perpignan. The mayor married them and made a speech in which he thanked Mary for all that she had done for the city of Perpignan. All the schoolchildren of the city helped gift Mary a magnificent basket of flowers, which was the main decoration at the banquet that followed the ceremony.

So, this was the end of Mary's work that had begun all those years ago, when she left London to go to Gibraltar with Lady Young. It is said that the mayor of Perpignan wanted Mary to be awarded the French Legion of Honour, the highest award anyone can receive for services to France and the French people. But Mary would not accept this. She said that she had only done what anybody would do. She never spoke to anyone of how she had saved so many lives and brought hope and happiness to so many others.

*   *   *

Even though Mary never spoke to anyone about the work that she did, she never forgot about the many children she had met over the years.

*   *   *

She always remembered the Spanish refugees and their families trying to keep warm on those windswept beaches in the middle of winter. She treasured the gifts they had made and given to her. There were beautiful paintings addressed to 'Miss Mary' and a figure of a deer carved from a piece of bone.

* * *

Mary often thought of Tato, the little boy who had been found wandering on a battlefield. She must have thought of poor Pepe, too, for she still had the New Year's Day card he had made for her. She didn't know what had happened to Charlotte, or to Ronald and Michael, but she must have wondered about them, and all the others she helped to save.

* * *

The years went by. Mary and her husband Roger had two children of their own, Caroline and Patrick. She lived to a great age – she was 93 when she died in 2002. By then, Mary's kindness had been completely forgotten about in Perpignan, the city where she had done so much work. And in Ireland, her home country, no one knew of her at all.

But all that was to change.

# CHAPTER ELEVEN

# REMEMBERING MARY TODAY

MARY'S CHILDREN WERE VERY SAD when she passed away, but they soon found all the papers and objects that Mary had kept from her time saving the children. They realised that Mary must have done many things that they knew very little about. Now she was gone they would never know the full truth of what had happened in camps like Rivesaltes. But one day, they received an email from someone in America.

Do you remember the two little boys, Michael and Ronald, who Mary rescued from the camp of Rivesaltes all those years ago? Ronald settled in America, where he eventually became a professor of psychology. After he retired, he began to wonder about the person who rescued him. He was not quite three years old at the time, so he couldn't remember anything at all about his rescue. He began to make some enquiries, but at first he didn't seem to be getting anywhere.

Then he learned that his rescuer was called Mary Elmes and that she worked for the American Quakers. He teamed up with a researcher in England, who was able to get a copy of the American Quakers' archives, and eventually they found Mary's two grown-up children in France. They also found the evidence they needed to prove that Mary had risked her life to save not only Ronald and Michael but hundreds of other children as well. It was Ronald who wrote to Mary's two children. He said to them:

＊　●　＊

There is no doubt that we are alive because of your mother's deed ... I only regret that I had not begun this search earlier so that I could have met your mother personally and thanked her.

＊　●　＊

There is an organisation in Jerusalem that honours all those who are not Jewish but who have risked their lives to save those who are.

On 13 January 2013 this organisation, called Yad Vashem, recognised Mary Elmes as:

 ● 

# 'Righteous Among the Nations'

 ● 

There was a wonderful ceremony held in Canet Plage, near Perpignan, on 27 June 2014, where Mary had done so much of her work. All her family was there. The gold medal was presented to one of her great-grandchildren, and Ronald was there from America to meet the family of the woman who had saved his life. Of course, this event was reported in the local papers, and people began to know something of the story of this wonderful woman and what she had done in this part of France all those years ago. The two Mennonite women, who were in charge of the Villa Saint Christophe, were also given this award.

It took some time before news of Mary's kindness reached Ireland. Although *The Irish Times* carried an article about Mary the year before, it wasn't until 30 September 2016 that Ireland really began to take notice, that they now had the first Irish person to be recognised as 'Righteous', and that this was something they should be proud of. Network Ireland, an organisation of businesswomen, was holding its annual meeting in Cork, and Deirdre Waldron, the president, had chosen Mary Elmes for the 2016 Trish Murphy Award. This award recognises women who have done something really special for others. Mary's son, Patrick, was there, and so was Mark Elmes, a cousin of Mary's from

Monkstown, Cork, just a few miles away. Like so many of Mary's relations, he knew nothing of what she had done in Spain and in France. The Lord Mayor of Cork was there too, and the following day he invited Mary's son to a ceremony in the council chamber, where he presented Patrick with a silver brooch, and promised that he would find some way of honouring Mary in her city of Cork.

A new bridge was built over the river Lee in the centre of Cork. It was opened on 27 September 2019. It was named after Mary Elmes, and now everyone who crosses it – 11,000 pedestrians and cyclists every day – will be reminded of the wonderful Irish woman born in Cork all those years ago. A woman who gave up the prospect of a successful career in a peaceful Ireland, who risked her life in war-torn Spain and France to bring food and medical care, but above all, love and kindness to thousands of children and their parents. This bridge reminds people that Mary saved many children from certain death during the Holocaust.

\* \* \*

## WE SHOULD BE PROUD OF MARY ELMES.

The people in Perpignan remembered Mary Elmes at first, but when they grew old, she was forgotten. We cannot let this happen again. We need to keep talking and reading about her. And above all, we should try to follow her example.

Remember how she went back to France when she read about all the refugees huddled on the sands trying to find shelter from the cold wind and rain. Remember how she chose to continue working in the camps when she could have had an easy job in an office in Marseille. Mary's life was one of love and kindness, which she showed to all people, whatever their race or religion.

* ● *

There are many refugees today who could do with someone like Mary. What would she do if she were here in Ireland now? What can you do to keep the memory and the work of Miss Mary alive in Ireland today?

* ● *

# FURTHER READING

If you enjoyed reading about Mary Elmes and want to find out more about the Spanish Civil War, World War II or the Holocaust, you might like to read the following:

*Waiting for Anya* by Michael Morpurgo
*What Was the Holocaust?* by Gail Herman
*Who Was Anne Frank?* by Ann Abramson

You might also like to check out the website kids.kiddle.co, an online encyclopaedia you can search for subjects mentioned in this book, including the Spanish Civil War, the

Holocaust, Vichy France and the Religious Society of Friends.

When you are older, you might like to read some other books about Mary Elmes, such as *A Time to Risk All* by Clodagh Finn and *The Extraordinary Story of Mary Elmes* by Paddy Butler.

# TIMELINE

1908   Mary is born in Ballintemple, Cork.

1925   Mary spends a year near Paris learning French.

1931   Mary spends time in Madrid learning Spanish.

1932   Mary graduates from Trinity College, Dublin.

1935   Mary graduates from the London School of Economics.

1936   The Spanish Civil War begins.

1937  Mary travels to Gibraltar on the SS *Otranto* with Lady Young.

1938  Mary's father, Edward, passes away.

Mary opens a hospital in the mountains near Polop, where the injured Palmira is brought to recover.

1939  Half a million Spanish refugees attempt to cross the Pyrenees in terrible weather.

World War II begins.

Mary accepts a job in Perpignan to help child refugees in Spain.

1940  France is invaded by German forces.

1941  Rivesaltes camp opens and Mary begins working there.

1942  Francine writes to Mary to thank her for the treats.

Mary takes Ronald and Michael Freund from Rivesaltes to safety.

Charlotte's mother is taken from Rivesaltes by train to the death camps, while Mary takes Charlotte to the Villa Saint Christophe.

German troops and tanks move into the south of France.

1943  Mary is arrested and taken to prison.

Mary is released and returns to work in Perpignan.

1944  Mary continues to work in Perpignan, helping refugees and

looking after the children she
has hidden.

1945   World War II ends in Europe.

1946   Mary leaves her work with the
Quakers and gets married to
Roger Danjou in the town hall
of Perpignan.

Mary receives the news that her
mother has died.

Mary has her first child, a daughter
named Caroline.

1947   Mary is thanked by the mayor of
Perpignan for all the work she
has done.

1948   Mary has her second child, a son
named Patrick.

# TIMELINE

2002   Mary dies in Perpignan, aged 93 – the Irish hero nobody had ever heard about!

2010   Ronald Freund writes to an English researcher who helps him make contact with Mary's family.

2013   Yad Vashem of Jerusalem recognises Mary Elmes as 'Righteous Among the Nations'.

2014   Mary's family is presented with a 'Righteous Among the Nations' medal in Canet Plage, France.

2019   The Mary Elmes Bridge in Cork city officially opens.

# ACKNOWLEDGEMENTS

It has been a great pleasure to work with Paddy Butler and Clodagh Finn, who have both written wonderful accounts of the life of Mary Elmes. They were able to do so much more than I could have done, with their professional experience, knowledge of France and their command of the French language. They have acknowledged, in their books, the help that we have all received from many sources, so there is no need for me to repeat them here.

It seemed to me there was need for another book about Mary, this time aimed at

# ACKNOWLEDGEMENTS

young children. I wrote a couple of chapters and sent them to Clodagh, who responded with such enthusiasm that I was encouraged to carry on and finish this small book.

I must thank my own family for all their support, especially, of course, my wife, Janet, who has been with me through all the years of research which predated this.

I would like to thank Caroline Danjou and her brother, Dr Patrick Danjou, the children of Mary Elmes, for allowing a perfect stranger to write about their mother. We are strangers no longer! Another member of the Elmes family, Mark Elmes of Cork, has been a great help too, welcoming us into his home and making arrangements to celebrate the opening of the Mary Elmes Bridge in Cork.

Thanks, also, to illustrator Julia Castaño, for bringing my words to life.

Finally, I should like to thank the staff of Gill Books for their help in making this book possible, in particular Deirdre Nolan and Seán Hayes, who have guided me through a process which was a completely new experience.

# ABOUT THE AUTHOR

**Bernard S. Wilson** is a retired university lecturer who lives with his wife in Canterbury. For seven years he undertook the research which eventually led to the discovery that Mary Elmes saved hundreds of Jewish children from deportation, at the risk of her own life. He is overjoyed that Mary Elmes is now getting the recognition she deserves.